Getting To Know...

Nature's Children

LIONS

Elizabeth MacLeod

SCHOLASTIC INC.

New York Toronto London Auckland Sydney
Mexico City New Delhi Hong Kong Buenos Aires

Facts in Brief

Classification of the Lion

Class: *Mammalia* (mammals)

Order: *Carnivora* (carnivores)

Family: *Felidae* (cat family)

Genus: *Panthera*

Species: *Panthera leo*

World distribution.   Africa and India.

Habitat.   Plains and lightly forested areas.

Distinctive physical characteristics.   A large member of the cat family, tawny fur, males are distinguished by their large manes.

Habits.   Live in groups called prides consisting of a dominant male and a number of females and young; most active at night.

Diet.   Large grazing animals such as zebras and antelopes.

Published by Scholastic Inc.
90 Old Sherman Turnpike, Danbury, Connecticut 06816.

SCHOLASTIC and associated logos are trademarks of Scholastic Inc.

ISBN 0-7172-6694-X   Printed in the U.S.A.

Edited by: Elizabeth Grace Zuraw   *Photo Editor:* Nancy Norton
Photo Rights: Ivy Images   *Cover Design*: Niemand Design

Words To Know

Bamboo A giant tropical grass with woody, hollow stems and hard, thick joints from which branches sprout.

Carnivore Literally, "meat eater." Scientists classify animals as belonging to the order *Carnivora* (carnivores) on the basis of various physical characteristics. Pandas have these characteristics and are therefore classified as carnivores even though they rarely eat meat.

Den Animal home.

Diameter A straight line passing through the center of a circle from one side to the other.

Esophagus The tube through which food passes from the mouth to the stomach.

Gland A part of an animal's body that makes and gives out a substance.

Home range The area that an animal regularly travels.

Mate To come together to produce young. Either member of an animal pair is also the other's mate.

Order A grouping used in classifying animals and plants. An order is smaller than a *class* and larger than a *family*.

Territory Area that an animal (or group of animals) lives in and often defends from other animals of the same kind. An animal may have a *home range* much larger than its *territory*.

INDEX

Cover Photo: Zig Leszczynski (Animals, Animals)

Photo Credits: Robert C. Simpson (Valan Photos), pages 4, 18, 45; Mark Sherman (Bruce Coleman Inc.), page 9; Peter Richardson (The Stock Market, Inc.), page 10; Bill Ivy, page 13; D. De Mello (New York Zoological Society), pages 14, 42; Bill Meng (New York Zoological Society), pages 17, 31, 32; Norman Myers (Bruce Coleman Inc.), pages 20-21; Zig Leszczynski (Animals, Animals), pages 23, 28; Gordon J. Fisher (The Stock Market, Inc.), page 24; Y.R. Tymstra (Valan Photos), page 27; Metro Toronto Zoo, page 34; Greg Locke (The Stock Market, Inc.), page 37; Chris Elliott (World Wildlife Federation), page 38; Zhu Jing (World Wildlife Federation), page 41; George B. Schaller, page 46.

Illustration page 7: Marianne Collins

Have you ever wondered . . .

A male lion stands proudly and thunders out his mighty roar. With his thick mane, strong muscles and powerful voice, he truly is a regal animal. It is no wonder the lion has come to be known as the "king of the beasts."

All lions roar, but nobody is quite sure why. Some scientists think it is to tell other lions, "Keep out! This is my home!" Other scientists think lions roar to call their family together, to frighten enemies and prey, or maybe even just for fun. What do you think? Perhaps you will have some other ideas after you have had a chance to find out more about lions and their families.

On a quiet day a lion's roar carries quite a distance.

Cuddly Cubs

It will be a long time before these cubs can roar! Lion cubs are very tiny when they are born and their mother must take good care of them. She guards her young ones carefully and keeps them clean by licking them with her long, rough tongue. The babies nurse on her rich milk and grow quickly.

The young ones spend much of their time playing in the sun with the other cubs. But they aren't just having fun. As they wrestle and tumble, they're also learning and practicing the skills they will need to be successful hunters.

Young lions look a lot like kittens.

Big Cats, Little Cats

Lions belong to the cat family, just like tigers, lynx and even your pet cat! This family has many members and no matter how big or small they are, they have a lot in common. All have soft fur to keep them warm and protected, as well as thick pads on their paws so they can creep silently through woods or grasses.

Cats are very sure-footed. Many are almost as at home in the trees as on the ground! They move quickly through the branches, using their tails to help them keep their balance.

All cats except cheetahs can pull their claws into little pockets in their toes. This keeps the claws out of the way when the cats don't need them and also helps to keep the claws razor sharp.

Despite its size a lion may climb a tree to sleep or to escape swarms of insects on the ground.

Lion Country

There are seven different kinds of lions and six of them live in Africa. One small group lives on a specially protected reserve in India.

It might surprise you to learn that while most lions live in Africa today, they once lived as far north as Europe and England. As forests grew and spread in those areas, lions moved south because they prefer to live on open plains. Now most lions make their homes in the grasslands of Africa, especially eastern Africa, wherever the grasses and shrubs are tall enough to hide them while they stalk their prey. But lions have also been seen at the snowy tops of mountains, where their warm coats and thick paw pads protect them from the cold.

Opposite page:
Sunbathing.

The shaded area on this map shows where lions live.

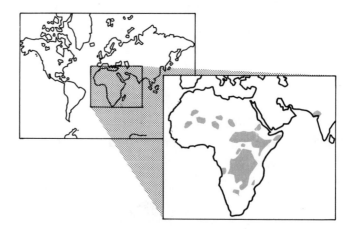

10

We Live Here!

Lions live in groups called "prides" and each pride has its own territory. The bigger the pride, then the bigger the territory those lions call home. If there isn't a lot of prey in the area, the lions may need to travel very far to find food. The farther they travel, the larger their territory will become. How large? Territories may range anywhere in size from a small town to a medium-sized city.

The male lions guard the pride's territory. They patrol the boundaries, roaring or leaving their scent by spraying the trees and ground with urine. Often one pride's territory will overlap the territory of another, but each pride has a central area that is all its own.

Of all the cats only lions live and hunt in prides.

Big Hunters

The lion is the biggest cat in Africa. In fact, in the whole world there is only one cat that is bigger—the tiger. A male lion may be as long as a small car and can weigh 180 kilograms (400 pounds), or about six times as much as you weigh. Female lions are somewhat smaller.

Lions depend on their large size to give them extra strength while hunting. Their powerful legs are designed for jumping and running and to give the lion an extra burst of speed when necessary. Lions can also freeze motionless for a long time without getting stiff and tired, which is very important when the lion is stalking its dinner.

A king and his territory!

Camouflage Cat

Crouching completely motionless in the grass, a lion is almost invisible. That thick coat of yellowish-gray fur blends perfectly with the dried shrubs and grasses. A lion's coat has no stripes or spots, since a plain coat is the best disguise for this grassland hunter.

But a lion is not plain yellow all over. Underneath, on its stomach, a lion's coat is white. And its tail tuft, lips, nose, and the back of its ears are black. These dark markings may help lions find each other while they prowl through tall grasses. Some scientists also think that the black lips and nose make it easier for lions to see each other's facial expressions so they can communicate better.

Do you see those spots on this lion's upper lip where its whiskers are? No other lion has exactly the same pattern of spots. Whisker spots are as unique to each lion as finger prints are to people.

Tell-tale spots.

What a Mane!

It is easy to tell a male lion from any other cat. Why? It is the only one with a mane. Only male lions grow manes but it is not until they are about five years old that they have a long, thick, full mane like this one. Some types of lions have a very light-colored mane, some have reddish brown manes, while others have almost black manes.

The mane does more than just make the lion look kingly. It also makes it look bigger. This helps frighten away other males and prevents fights. But if two males do fight, their manes protect them from bites and scratches to their heads and necks.

The lion is also the only cat with a large dark tuft of hair on its tail. Both males and females are born with this tuft, although it is not very obvious in cubs. Baby lions seem to think adults' tail tufts are there just for them to play with and pounce on.

Opposite page: *The lion is the only cat in the world with a mane.*

Super Senses

All cats have good eyesight and hearing and lions are no exception. They hunt by sight and sound and they usually hunt at night. Can you guess why? The darkness makes it difficult for their prey to spot them. But lions have no trouble padding around in the dark because their eyes are specially developed to see at night. The pupils in their eyes open wide to gather in all possible light. During the day, however, when the sun is strong and bright, the pupils close to tiny circles to protect the eyes.

Those long, stiff whiskers also help lions move about in the dark. They are very sensitive and warn the lion of anything in its path.

The lion's keen eyes can see much further than yours.

Pride Life

You might think of a pride of lions as a large family—a very large family. There may be as many as 30 lions in the group: 1 to 6 males and 4 to 12 females along with their cubs. The females look after each other's cubs and hunt together. If a lion in the pride is sick or hurt, the other lions will bring it food.

Most of the females in a pride are somehow related. They may be mothers, aunts, sisters, nieces or daughters, since female cubs tend to stay with the same pride. But there's only room for a few males in each pride, so when the male cubs grow up they usually leave to join other prides or start their own.

A lot of mouths to feed.

Ya-a-a-a-awn!

How do you think lions spend most of their
day? Hunting? Patrolling? Roaring?

Did you guess sleeping? Lions love to cat
nap and they spend up to 21 hours a day
resting. When they are feeling really lazy, they
will doze in the shade of the same tree all day,
getting up only to follow the shade as the sun
moves across the sky. Even when it is very
hot, the pride members like to be close to each
other. They flop down back to back or drape
a paw over the shoulder of a neighbor.

Lions don't always sleep on the ground.
Sprawling along a tree branch may look
uncomfortable to you, but a lion will doze
there happily with its head and legs dangling
down.

Cat nap.

Keeping in Touch

Lions love to touch each other. One of their favorite ways is by rubbing their heads against other pride members. For instance, when a mother lion returns from a hunt, her cubs will rush to meet her and will rub their heads against her cheek, side, legs, or whatever part of her is closest. Adults will rub heads, too, just to be friendly and to show they are part of the pride. Often just before a pride goes hunting, they will all rub heads, almost as if they were giving each other a pep talk!

Licking is another way that lions show they belong. Of course, mothers lick their babies to keep them clean, but adults will lick each other as well. A female will also give her cubs a lick or two just because she's feeling affectionate. But she has to be careful: her tongue is so powerful that she may accidentally knock down one of her cubs!

Purr-fect pair.

Hums, Grunts and Miaows

Lions also keep in touch by making sounds. A roar is definitely the loudest noise they can make, but it is not the only one. Lions also growl, hum, grunt and moan to communicate with each other. When they are sharing dinner, they may hiss and snarl if they think another lion is taking too much. If they're full and happy they may even purr! But a lion can't purr continually, like your cat can. Why? Because its throat is specially developed for roaring, and so it can only purr when it breathes out.

When a lioness returns to her pride after being away for a time, she will greet the other lionesses with low, soft calls, almost like moans. She may also call her cubs to her with quiet grunts. If her babies want to nurse, she'll lie back and hum contentedly while they bleat and miaow as they get in each other's way. By the time the cubs are about one month old, they can make all the sounds the adults make—except roar.

Opposite page: *Not only male lions roar, females do too, but in a higher pitch.*

On the Hunt

Lions can't run nearly as fast as most of the animals they hunt, so they have to work hard to catch their dinner. Their favorite prey are zebras, wildebeest and antelope, but they will also hunt wart hogs, hippos, giraffes and even elephants. Sometimes they will even gobble up an unsuspecting rat, mouse or snake.

Usually lions hunt at night or in the early morning. Lionesses do most of the hunting. The males are slower and more clumsy, and their huge mane makes it difficult for them to creep close to prey without being seen.

Despite their camouflage coat and careful stalking, lions go hungry many more times than they are able to catch any dinner. But when they hunt in teams, they are much more successful.

After a hunt lions get very thirsty!

Teamwork

Silently, two lionesses stalk a herd of antelope. They slowly creep closer and closer, carefully hiding behind shrubs and slinking through the grasses. Meanwhile, three other lionesses from their pride are already hiding in the bushes on the other side of the herd.

Suddenly, the two lionesses rush at the antelope. The frightened animals wheel around and race away—right towards the three waiting lionesses.

That's just one of the ways that lions work together to hunt prey. Another way is for some of the lions in the pride to stand in the open where the prey can see them. That distracts the animals so that other lions can creep close enough from another direction to rush at them.

Dinner Time

Have you ever heard the expression "the lion's share"? It means the biggest portion and that's what the top male in the pride usually eats when a hunt is successful. Sometimes the lionesses will kill their prey and eat it up. Other times, if the male is nearby, he will claim their prey and gobble it down. That seems unfair since the lionesses did all the work, but they depend on the male for protection from other prides and so they must feed him. The females may wait until he's finished eating in case there's any food left or they may leave and hunt again. While the male eats his fill, he may let the cubs join him.

Lions have no flat teeth for chewing like you do, so they have to swallow their food in chunks that they cut off with their sharp front teeth. They can eat more than 23 kilograms (50 pounds) of meat at once—that's as much as 200 hamburgers. What a feast! But since catching dinner is so hard, they don't get to eat every day.

Opposite page:
Since lions mainly catch weaker animals, they help to keep the herds healthy.

Courting Lions

Lions can mate at any time of year. A male will usually choose a female from his own pride and the pair will go off together for a few days while courting. They usually stay in one place, even though the rest of the pride continues to hunt throughout the territory.

Courting lions hunt very little, although sometimes the male will catch an animal and present it to the female. He may also try to impress his mate by chasing away other lions who come too close.

After the lions have mated, they return to their pride. In a little over three months, the female will begin looking for a safe, dry place to have her cubs.

A Den Full of Babies

When lion cubs are born, their soft, woolly coats are covered in spots and they are helpless and blind. But within a day they can crawl and soon their eyes open. Like most baby cats, the cubs have gray-blue eyes. It will be two to three months before their eyes turn the same color as their mother's, and it will be about a year before they lose the spots on their coats.

There are usually two to four cubs in a litter and their mother is kept very busy looking after them. They depend on her milk to help them grow. However, sometimes she will leave her babies for a day while she tries to find food for herself.

When the cubs are about three weeks old, their teeth start to come in. That means they will soon be ready to gobble up any meat that their mother brings back to them.

The spots on this cub's coat will remain visible until it is fully grown. However, they will fade with age.

In the Pride

The lioness introduces her babies to the pride when the young ones are about six weeks old. How frightening the big males must look! Soon, however, the cubs feel right at home and if their mother is away hunting, they may nurse from one of the other females in the pride.

The babies love to imitate the males and will practice yawning, stalking and sharpening their claws, just like the adults. If the males aren't too hungry or grumpy, they may playfight with the cubs. But if the cubs get too rough, a hiss or grimace will tell them, "That's enough!"

The cubs will then play among themselves, stalking each other, swatting and slapping with their paws or playing tug-of-war with a stick or twig. Then they may attack a lioness, leaping on her or draping themselves over her face so she can hardly breathe. The poor adults don't get much sleep when the babies want to play! But all these games help the cubs' muscles develop and let them practice hunting techniques.

Opposite page:
Yeow!

Hunting Lessons

The cubs have a lot to learn about catching
their dinner and their lessons begin as soon as
they join the pride. If the whole pride goes
hunting, the babies will often go too,
bounding along playfully behind the lionesses,
who are alert and watching for prey. The
males come last, keeping an eye on the cubs.
At first, the babies are very clumsy. Although
they seem to know instinctively how to stalk
and herd their prey, they must be taught how
to attack it.

By the time the cubs are a year old they are
able to hunt for themselves. However, they
still can use help from mom and will hunt with
her for at least another year.

*These cubs still have a lot to learn
before they can look after
themselves.*

Moving On

When the lion cubs are about two years old,
their mother is ready to have another family.
By the time they are three, the male cubs may
be forced out of the pride. The female cubs
are usually allowed to remain and raise their
own families but a young male must join
another pride or find his own territory. It's
not easy, but his mother has made sure that he
knows how to hunt and has learned all the
skills he will need to grow up to be "king of
the beasts."

Words To Know

Camouflage Colors and patterns that help an animal blend in with its surroundings.

Cubs Baby lions.

Lioness Female lion.

Mane Long fur that grows around the heads of male lions.

Mate To come together to produce young. Either member of an animal pair is also the other's mate.

Nurse To drink milk from a mother's body.

Prey An animal that is hunted by another for food.

Pride A group of lions, usually a male with several females and their young.

Stalk To sneak up on prey.

Territory Area that an animal (or group of animals) lives in and often defends from other animals of the same kind.

INDEX

Getting To Know...

Nature's Children

PANDAS

Merebeth Switzer

SCHOLASTIC INC.

New York   Toronto   London   Auckland   Sydney
Mexico City   New Delhi   Hong Kong   Buenos Aires

Facts in Brief

Classification of the Giant Panda

Class: *Mammalia* (mammals)
Order: *Carnivora* (carnivores)
Family: *Procyonidae** (raccoon family)
Genus: *Ailuropoda*
Species: *Ailuropoda melanoleuca*

* Many scientists disagree, but at present this is still the classification usually given.

World distribution. Central China near Tibet border.

Habitat. Bamboo forests at altitudes of 6500–11,500 feet (2000–3500 meters)

Distinctive physical characteristics. Striking black-and-white markings; bear-like shape; extra digit on forepaws used like a thumb.

Habits. Solitary; establishes territory by scent markings; active day and night, alternating periods of feeding and resting.

Diet. Chiefly bamboo. Other vegetable matter and meat make up less then 1 percent of the panda's diet.

Published by Scholastic Inc.
90 Old Sherman Turnpike, Danbury, Connecticut 06816.

SCHOLASTIC and associated logos are trademarks of Scholastic Inc.

ISBN 0-7172-6694-X

Printed in the U.S.A.

Have you ever wondered . . .

What is black and white and loved all over? The Giant Panda, of course! Each year, millions of people travel to see these extraordinary animals at the few zoos where they are on display.

Why are we "panda crazy"? Perhaps because the round furry pandas look so cuddly and are so amusing to watch as they lumber lazily around or playfully turn somersaults. Sometimes they'll even stop in the middle of the roll and hold the position for a while.

But pandas are not simply cute. They are amazing animals and until recently their life was full of secrets. Join us now as we unravel the mystery of one of the world's most popular animals.

In a Quiet Forest

In a dense bamboo forest a panda sits, leaning back against a tree surrounded by the dark green of the forest. She has something cradled in her arm, something that she is gently stroking with her large paw. Why, it's a baby panda!

The panda cub is about ten weeks old. It was tiny, naked and completely helpless at birth, but it is growing quickly and already has a coat of fine white and black fur. Its eyes have opened, and soon it will be ready to take its first unsteady steps.

For now, however, the baby panda is content to snuggle against its mother's warm body and peacefully nurse on her rich milk. The cub has a lot more growing to do, and its mother will be very busy caring for it during the months to come.

A Bamboo Forest Home

Pandas live in central China near the border of Tibet. They make their home in bamboo forests high in the mountains where it is always very cool. Even in summer the temperature seldom rises above that of a nice spring day, about 15°C (60°F).

Not only is this dense wilderness cool, it is also very rainy and shrouded in cloud and fog for most of the year. Snow falls from late November to early April.

The panda is not completely alone in the forest, nor is bamboo the only thing that grows there. Deer, leopards, monkeys and Lesser Pandas pad through the bamboo. And hardy evergreen trees, such as dragon spruce, spider pine, fir and hemlock, also thrive in this cool, damp climate.

Although some pandas can be found lower down or higher up, most make their homes at altitudes of 2000–3000 metres (7000–10,000 feet).

Animal of Mystery

The Giant Panda has always been very rare. And its lonely forest home and secret ways mean that few people have known the panda firsthand. Chinese farmers that live near the panda have stories dating back centuries. They call the panda *beishung,* a word that means "white bear."

The panda was a mystery to the western world until the 1920s. The first live panda was brought to North America in 1936, and even today only a few zoos outside China are home to the Giant Pandas.

Perhaps one of the most mysterious things about the Giant Panda is its name, because it isn't really a giant at all. It is only about one metre (3 feet) tall from the ground to the top of its back. And it would take more than 30 of these "giants" to tip the scale with an elephant.

Pandas love water and may drink until their tummies bloat.

11

*The Lesser Panda
looks more like a
raccoon or a cat
than it does like
its famous black
and white
relative.*

The Lesser Panda

Perhaps the explanation of the Giant Panda's
name lies in the existence of a much more
common but much smaller relative, the Lesser
Panda. Also known as the Red Panda because
of its soft, thick, chestnut-colored coat, the
Lesser Panda too lives in the bamboo forests of
the Himalayan Mountains. Its range, however,
is not nearly as restricted as that of the Giant
Panda.

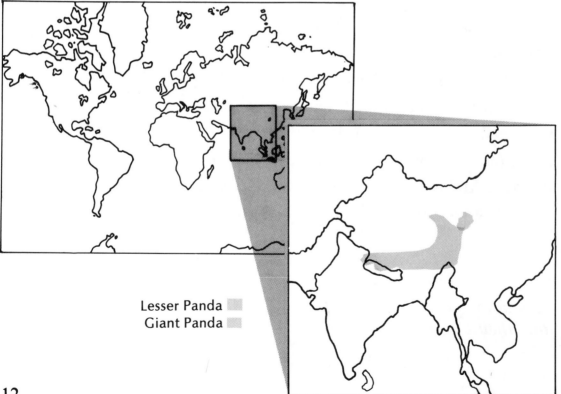

Lesser Panda
Giant Panda

Figuring Out the Family

Although scientists have recently spent a great deal of time learning about the Giant Panda, they still disagree about the panda's family tree.

To understand the problem, we need to look more closely at the Red Panda. The Red Panda looks like a red raccoon. It even has a raccoon-like mask and rings on its bushy tail. Some scientists think these pandas are very close cousins to the Giant Panda and classify both as members of the raccoon family.

Many other scientists, however, looking at the Giant Panda's bear-like features, believe that this panda is more closely related to bears. Finally a third group of scientists think that the Red and the Giant Pandas deserve to be placed in their own special "panda" group.

Black and White and Warm All Over

When you are looking at pictures of animals, you may have trouble knowing for sure whether you are seeing an elk or a cariboo, a cheetah or a leopard. But you always know a panda when you see one.

People often wonder whether any purpose is served by the distinctive black and white pattern of the panda's fur. No one can know for sure, but one theory is that it helps pandas keep out of each other's way. Pandas are loners and definitely prefer to meet as little as possible. Their eyesight, however, is rather poor. It is thought that their sharply contrasting coloration may make it easier for them to spot one another in time to avoid unwelcome encounters.

Whatever the reason for its color scheme, the panda's coat is wonderfully suited to its cool, damp mountain home. Thick and oily, it keeps the panda warm and dry through all kinds of weather.

Bamboo for Breakfast, Lunch and Dinner

Over 99% of the panda's diet is bamboo. But because bamboo is 90% water, it is not very nourishing. What's more, the panda's digestive system is not very efficient. This means that the panda must spend a lot of time eating. And it does. In fact, a panda spends anywhere from 10 to 16 hours every day feasting on 10 to 15 kilograms (20 to 30 pounds) of this tough plant!

What is this food that pandas find so tasty? Bamboo is a type of giant woody grass that can grow to be taller than most people and even as big as some small trees. Bamboo is very tough and strong. In fact, its dried stalks are used to make furniture. Perhaps you have sat in a bamboo chair yourself.

The rough, straight stalks of bamboo have ring-like bumps all along their length. Branches grow from these bumps and leaves sprout along the branches. The panda prefers the bamboo leaves, but it also eats the stem, sometimes pulling off pieces of outer fibrous "bark" to snack on the tender insides.

Opposite page:
Pandas usually sit upright while feeding.

Sometimes Snacks

People say that "variety is the spice of life." A panda might agree, but would add that a little spice goes a long, long way.

Sometimes, when it is wanting a treat or when food is scarce, a panda will munch on vines, grasses and even wild roots such as parsnips. Occasionally it will eat meat as well. (In fact, for various reasons, scientists classify pandas in the order of carnivores, that is, meat-eaters.) But since it is not a good hunter it must make do with the leftovers of a leopard's hunting trip. The panda also has a sweet tooth and a reputation for robbing village beehives for a sweet treat of honey.

Still, these various sources of food won't fill up a panda and it cannot live on these alone. Without bamboo the panda cannot survive.

For a panda, anytime is mealtime.

Hard Times

The bamboo forests where pandas live are dotted throughout central China. Each forest has at least one type of bamboo growing in it, and in some there are three or four. Pandas eat whatever types of bamboo grow in their particular forest, and as we have seen, they eat very little else. This occasionally creates a serious problem for the panda.

Bamboo plants grow by sending up new green shoots from their roots each spring. This means that every year millions of new stems are produced. But after some years—it may be 15 or it may be 100, depending on the type—the bamboo stops growing. Instead, it sprouts flowers which form seeds and then the whole plant dies. The seeds fall to the ground and begin the long process of developing into new plants. It takes at least two years for new bamboo plants to grow. So if only one kind of bamboo grows in that particular forest, the pandas living there are without their most important food for a very long time.

Opposite page:
While they spend most of their time on the ground, pandas sometimes climb trees for shelter or refuge.

Opposite page:
The next time you eat Chinese food think of this: the crunchy vegetable you are enjoying may be the same bamboo that pandas love.

The Panda's Thumb

Try spending the entire day without using your thumb. You'll be surprised at how important it is to have one. Without a thumb, it's very difficult to write a letter, peel an orange, pick up a penny or even steer a bike. A panda doesn't need to do any of these things, but it does need its thumb to eat. In fact, without this marvelous tool, the panda might starve.

To understand why the panda's thumb is so special let's look at how it works. On each of its front paws, a panda has five fingers *plus* a thumb—which is really one of its wrist bones. You can feel this bone in your own wrist: it is the large bump where your arm and hand meet.

In a panda, this bone has become very long with extra nerves and muscles that help it to work properly. Once the panda's five fingers have grabbed a stalk of bamboo, it jams it up against its thumb-like wrist bone. With the bamboo "locked" into its paw, the panda can begin to eat without fear of dropping its meal.

Thumb

Panda's front paw.

26

Crunching a Tough Meal

Bamboo is a tough plant, but the panda is well equipped to eat it. The panda's powerful jaws cut off a broom-handle-thick stalk of bamboo in one mighty crunch. Then the panda sits back on its haunches, strips off the parts it does not want to eat, and begins to munch. It takes only seconds for the panda's big flat teeth to grind up and crush an entire bamboo stalk. Then it's on to the next . . .

Bamboo splinters are very sharp but the panda is well protected against their piercing points. The inside walls of the panda's esophagus—the tube leading from its mouth to its stomach—are extra strong and resist damage from the needle-sharp bamboo.

A panda can chew through bamboo stems 4 centimetres (1.5 inches) thick.

Snacking and Snoozing

Pandas don't keep regular hours, nor do they have a regular resting place. They spend much of their time both day and night munching their way around their territory. When they feel tired, they simply flop themselves down for a snooze wherever they happen to be.

If the weather is very bad a panda may seek out the shelter of a cave or a hollow old tree stump. But most of the time it is perfectly happy sleeping in the open—especially in the middle of a stand of bamboo. That way it doesn't have to move if it wants a mid-snooze snack.

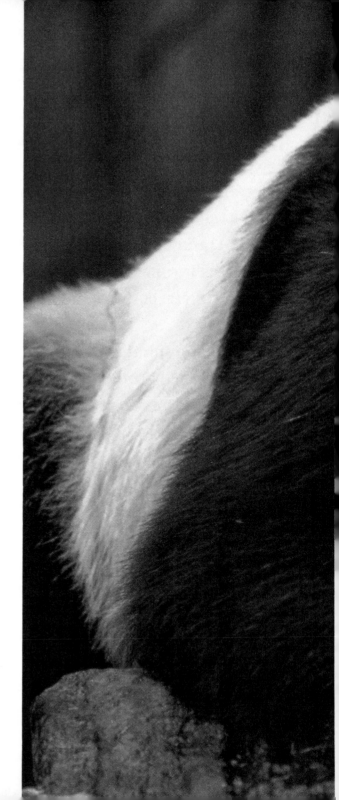

Nap time.

Rambling and Rolling

If you have ever seen a panda walking with its pigeon-toed, rolling gait, you will know that it doesn't move very quickly. A panda spends most of its life within its "home range"—an area that is about two to three kilometres (1 to 2 miles) in diameter. But because it stops so frequently to sit and eat, a panda usually only covers an area about the size of a football field each day.

Sometimes a panda may roam farther afield if food is scarce or if it is in search of a mate.

Pandas are seldom in a hurry.

Panda Signposts

Pandas live alone in their bamboo forest and they prefer it that way. However they do have several ways to leave messages for other pandas. Like some forest animals, such as the bear or the lynx, pandas rake their claws on the trunks of trees. This scrapes off large sections of bark and leaves the message "Panda at home."

Pandas also leave "scent" messages. Each panda has glands near the base of its stubby little tail. These glands contain a strong smelling "panda perfume." By rubbing its bottom against a rock or piece of ground, the panda lets other pandas know it's been around.

Pandas are usually quiet but when they meet one another they are very noisy. They make bear-like grunts and moans, and bleating sounds a bit like a cross between the *moo* of a cow and the *baa* of a sheep. Baby pandas call for their mother's attention with a loud, high-pitched squawk.

Opposite page:
Although pandas look cute and cuddly, they can defend themselves very well when threatened.

Finding a Mate

When spring arrives, a male panda sets out to seek a mate. Pandas usually find each other by calling, but the male is also helped in its search by any claw rakings or scent markings the female panda may have recently made. If two males come upon a female at the same time, they will often have mock battles and ''roaring contests.'' These last until one, generally the weaker, gives up and goes away.

Whether she has several suitors or just one, the female will usually play hard-to-get for a time. If the male is over-eager and comes too close before she has got used to him, she may slap or even bite him and take refuge up a tree. He might then have to wait several days for her to relent and accept his attentions.

Unless food is scarce, a panda will seldom leave its home range except in search of a mate.

A Cub is Born

The male panda leaves after mating. Three to five months later, the mother panda prepares a den in a rock cave or at the base of a tree. Here her tiny pink cub will be born, weighing not much more than a small apple.

The panda is a devoted mother. For the first few weeks of her cub's life she carries it wherever she goes, cradling it against her body to keep it warm. Once it is a bit bigger and its fur has grown in, she may carry it by its neck like a mother cat with her kitten. Now she sometimes tucks the cub safely into the hollow of a tree while she feeds nearby.

A panda is a loving mother and fiercely protective of her tiny cub.

Growing Up

The panda cub grows quickly but remains quite helpless for the first two months of its life. When it is three or four months old it starts to crawl. By the time it is seven months old it can run, climb trees and even eat bamboo.

Although a baby panda has no brothers or sisters to play with, it seems to be able to amuse itself anywhere. One panda was even seen sliding down a hill on its tummy and climbing back up to do it again. And like most mothers, the mother panda takes part in her baby's games and is always ready for a bit of roughhousing.

The mother keeps a close eye on her growing youngster. An adult panda has very few natural enemies but the small cub can fall prey to leopards or Asiatic wild dogs.

This panda cub has grown enormously since it was born four or five months ago. By the time it is a year old it will weigh about 25–35 kilograms (55–80 pounds), or more than 200 times what it did at birth.

Leaving Home

By the time the cub is nine months old it no longer needs its mother's milk. Nonetheless, it stays with her a bit longer.

Finally, however, even though it is not fully grown and still has a lot of weight to put on, the time comes for the young panda to leave and find its own territory. Young male pandas will wander quite far but young female pandas tend to stay closer to the mother's territory. In another four to six years, the young panda will be ready to start a family of its own.

Taking it easy.

Finding Out About Pandas

Because there are so few pandas in the world, the Chinese government has declared them a "national treasure" and established special reserves for them to live in safely. Recently scientists have spent time in these reserves to learn more about pandas.

Pandas live alone in very dense forests and are not easy to learn about. Researchers look for clawed tree trunks, fresh paw prints or trampled grass where a panda may have slept. Once they find a panda they trap it and give it a sedative so it falls asleep. They make sure it is healthy, weigh it and put a small radio collar around its neck.

By the time the panda wakes up it is free to wander away again, but the researchers can keep track of where it goes. This helps them to learn more about the size of the panda's territory and its daily movements.

The more we learn about pandas, the less likely we are to carelessly do them harm and the more we can help any that find themselves in trouble.